MW00911530

This Bucket List Journal

Belongs To:

_____

_____

_____

✓	PAGE #	BUCKET LIST	CATEGORY	TARGET DATE

✓	PAGE #	BUCKET LIST	CATEGORY	TARGET DATE

✓	PAGE #	BUCKET LIST	CATEGORY	TARGET DATE

✓	PAGE #	BUCKET LIST	CATEGORY	TARGET DATE

✓	PAGE #	BUCKET LIST	CATEGORY	TARGET DATE

✓	PAGE #	BUCKET LIST	CATEGORY	TARGET DATE

CATEGORY:_____ **DATE:**__/__/20__

BUCKET LIST:

TARGET DATE: __/__/20__   **DONE** ✓ ☐

DATE COMPLETED: __/__/20__

WHERE:

HOW:

EXPERIENCE:

COMMENTS AND NOTES:

CATEGORY:_____ **DATE:**__/__/20__

BUCKET LIST:

TARGET DATE: __/__/20__   **DONE** ✓ ☐

DATE COMPLETED: __/__/20__

WHERE:

HOW:

EXPERIENCE:

COMMENTS AND NOTES:

CATEGORY: _____ **DATE:** __/__/20__

BUCKET LIST:

TARGET DATE: __/__/20__   **DONE** ✓ ☐

DATE COMPLETED: __/__/20__

WHERE:

HOW:

EXPERIENCE:

COMMENTS AND NOTES:

CATEGORY:_____ DATE:__/__/20__

BUCKET LIST:

TARGET DATE: __/__/20__   **DONE** ✓ [ ]

DATE COMPLETED: __/__/20__

WHERE:

HOW:

EXPERIENCE:

COMMENTS AND NOTES:

CATEGORY:_____ **DATE:**__/__/20__

BUCKET LIST:

TARGET DATE: __/__/20__   **DONE** ✓ ☐

DATE COMPLETED: __/__/20__

WHERE:

HOW:

EXPERIENCE:

COMMENTS AND NOTES:

CATEGORY:_____ DATE:__/__/20__

BUCKET LIST:

TARGET DATE: __/__/20__   **DONE** ✓ [ ]

DATE COMPLETED: __/__/20__

WHERE:

HOW:

EXPERIENCE:

COMMENTS AND NOTES:

CATEGORY:_____ **DATE:**__/__/20__

BUCKET LIST:

TARGET DATE: __/__/20__   **DONE** ✓ [ ]

DATE COMPLETED: __/__/20__

WHERE:

HOW:

EXPERIENCE:

COMMENTS AND NOTES:

CATEGORY: _____ **DATE:** __/__/20__

BUCKET LIST:

TARGET DATE: __/__/20__   **DONE** ✓ ☐

DATE COMPLETED: __/__/20__

WHERE:

HOW:

EXPERIENCE:

COMMENTS AND NOTES:

CATEGORY: _____ **DATE:** __/__/20__

BUCKET LIST:

TARGET DATE: __/__/20__   **DONE** ✓ ☐

DATE COMPLETED: __/__/20__

WHERE:

HOW:

EXPERIENCE:

COMMENTS AND NOTES:

CATEGORY: _____ **DATE:** __/__/20__

BUCKET LIST:

TARGET DATE: __/__/20__   **DONE** ✓ [ ]

DATE COMPLETED: __/__/20__

WHERE:

HOW:

EXPERIENCE:

COMMENTS AND NOTES:

CATEGORY: _____ **DATE:** __/__/20__

BUCKET LIST:

TARGET DATE: __/__/20__   **DONE** ✓ ☐

DATE COMPLETED: __/__/20__

WHERE:

HOW:

EXPERIENCE:

COMMENTS AND NOTES:

CATEGORY: _____   **DATE:** __ / __ /20 __

BUCKET LIST:

TARGET DATE: __ / __ /20 __   **DONE** ✓ [ ]

DATE COMPLETED: __ / __ /20 __

WHERE:

HOW:

EXPERIENCE:

COMMENTS AND NOTES:

CATEGORY:_____ **DATE:**__/__/20__

BUCKET LIST:

TARGET DATE: __/__/20__   **DONE** ✓ [ ]

DATE COMPLETED: __/__/20__

WHERE:

HOW:

EXPERIENCE:

COMMENTS AND NOTES:

CATEGORY: _____ **DATE:** __/__/20__

BUCKET LIST:

TARGET DATE: __/__/20__   **DONE** ✓ ☐

DATE COMPLETED: __/__/20__

WHERE:

HOW:

EXPERIENCE:

COMMENTS AND NOTES:

CATEGORY:_____ **DATE:**__/__/20__

BUCKET LIST:

TARGET DATE: __/__/20__   **DONE** ✓ [ ]

DATE COMPLETED: __/__/20__

WHERE:

HOW:

EXPERIENCE:

COMMENTS AND NOTES:

CATEGORY:_____ **DATE:**__/__/20__

BUCKET LIST:

TARGET DATE: __/__/20__   **DONE** ✓ [ ]

DATE COMPLETED: __/__/20__

WHERE:

HOW:

EXPERIENCE:

COMMENTS AND NOTES:

CATEGORY:_____ **DATE:**__/__/20__

BUCKET LIST:

TARGET DATE: __/__/20__   **DONE** ✓ ☐

DATE COMPLETED: __/__/20__

WHERE:

HOW:

EXPERIENCE:

COMMENTS AND NOTES:

CATEGORY:_____ **DATE:**__/__/20__

BUCKET LIST:

TARGET DATE: __/__/20__   **DONE** ✓ ☐

DATE COMPLETED: __/__/20__

WHERE:

HOW:

EXPERIENCE:

COMMENTS AND NOTES:

CATEGORY:_____ **DATE:**__/__/20__

BUCKET LIST:

TARGET DATE: __/__/20__   **DONE** ✓ [ ]

DATE COMPLETED: __/__/20__

WHERE:

HOW:

EXPERIENCE:

COMMENTS AND NOTES:

CATEGORY: _____ **DATE:**__/__/20__

BUCKET LIST:

TARGET DATE: __/__/20__   **DONE** ✓ [ ]

DATE COMPLETED: __/__/20__

WHERE:

HOW:

EXPERIENCE:

COMMENTS AND NOTES:

CATEGORY: _____ **DATE:** __/__/20__

BUCKET LIST:

TARGET DATE: __/__/20__   **DONE** ✓ ☐

DATE COMPLETED: __/__/20__

WHERE:

HOW:

EXPERIENCE:

COMMENTS AND NOTES:

CATEGORY: _____ **DATE:** __/__/20__

BUCKET LIST:

TARGET DATE: __/__/20__   **DONE** ✓ [ ]

DATE COMPLETED: __/__/20__

WHERE:

HOW:

EXPERIENCE:

COMMENTS AND NOTES:

CATEGORY:_____ **DATE:**__/__/20__

BUCKET LIST:

TARGET DATE: __/__/20__   **DONE** ✓ [ ]

DATE COMPLETED: __/__/20__

WHERE:

HOW:

EXPERIENCE:

COMMENTS AND NOTES:

CATEGORY:_____ DATE:__/__/20__

BUCKET LIST:

TARGET DATE: __/__/20__   **DONE** ✓ ☐

DATE COMPLETED: __/__/20__

WHERE:

HOW:

EXPERIENCE:

COMMENTS AND NOTES:

CATEGORY: _____ **DATE:** __/__/20__

BUCKET LIST:

TARGET DATE: __/__/20__   **DONE** ✓ [ ]

DATE COMPLETED: __/__/20__

WHERE:

HOW:

EXPERIENCE:

COMMENTS AND NOTES:

CATEGORY: _____ **DATE:** __/__/20__

BUCKET LIST:

TARGET DATE: __/__/20__ **DONE** ✓ ☐

DATE COMPLETED: __/__/20__

WHERE:

HOW:

EXPERIENCE:

COMMENTS AND NOTES:

CATEGORY:_____ **DATE:**__/__/20__

BUCKET LIST:

TARGET DATE: __/__/20__   **DONE** ✓ [ ]

DATE COMPLETED: __/__/20__

WHERE:

HOW:

EXPERIENCE:

COMMENTS AND NOTES:

CATEGORY: _____ **DATE:** __/__/20__

BUCKET LIST:

TARGET DATE: __/__/20__   **DONE** ✓ [ ]

DATE COMPLETED: __/__/20__

WHERE:

HOW:

EXPERIENCE:

COMMENTS AND NOTES:

CATEGORY:_____ **DATE:**__/__/20__

BUCKET LIST:

TARGET DATE: __/__/20__   **DONE** ✓ ☐

DATE COMPLETED: __/__/20__

WHERE:

HOW:

EXPERIENCE:

COMMENTS AND NOTES:

CATEGORY: _____ **DATE:** __/__/20__

BUCKET LIST:

TARGET DATE: __/__/20__   **DONE** ✓ ☐

DATE COMPLETED: __/__/20__

WHERE:

HOW:

EXPERIENCE:

COMMENTS AND NOTES:

CATEGORY:_____ **DATE:**__/__/20__

BUCKET LIST:

TARGET DATE: __/__/20__   **DONE** ✓ [ ]

DATE COMPLETED: __/__/20__

WHERE:

HOW:

EXPERIENCE:

COMMENTS AND NOTES:

CATEGORY: _____ **DATE:** __/__/20__

BUCKET LIST:

TARGET DATE: __/__/20__   **DONE** ✓ ☐

DATE COMPLETED: __/__/20__

WHERE:

HOW:

EXPERIENCE:

COMMENTS AND NOTES:

CATEGORY: _____ **DATE:** __/__/20__

BUCKET LIST:

TARGET DATE: __/__/20__   **DONE** ✓ ☐

DATE COMPLETED: __/__/20__

WHERE:

HOW:

EXPERIENCE:

COMMENTS AND NOTES:

CATEGORY: _____ **DATE:** __/__/20__

BUCKET LIST:

TARGET DATE: __/__/20__   **DONE** ✓ ☐

DATE COMPLETED: __/__/20__

WHERE:

HOW:

EXPERIENCE:

COMMENTS AND NOTES:

CATEGORY:_____ **DATE:**__/__/20__

BUCKET LIST:

TARGET DATE: __/__/20__   **DONE** ✓ ☐

DATE COMPLETED: __/__/20__

WHERE:

HOW:

EXPERIENCE:

COMMENTS AND NOTES:

CATEGORY: _____   **DATE:** __/__/20__

BUCKET LIST:

TARGET DATE: __/__/20__   **DONE** ✓ [ ]

DATE COMPLETED: __/__/20__

WHERE:

HOW:

EXPERIENCE:

COMMENTS AND NOTES:

CATEGORY:_____ **DATE:**__/__/20__

BUCKET LIST:

TARGET DATE: __/__/20__   **DONE** ✓ ☐

DATE COMPLETED: __/__/20__

WHERE:

HOW:

EXPERIENCE:

COMMENTS AND NOTES:

CATEGORY:_____ **DATE:**__/__/20__

BUCKET LIST:

TARGET DATE: __/__/20__   **DONE** ✓ ☐

DATE COMPLETED: __/__/20__

WHERE:

HOW:

EXPERIENCE:

COMMENTS AND NOTES:

CATEGORY: _____ **DATE:** __/__/20__

BUCKET LIST:

TARGET DATE: __/__/20__   **DONE** ✓ ☐

DATE COMPLETED: __/__/20__

WHERE:

HOW:

EXPERIENCE:

COMMENTS AND NOTES:

CATEGORY: _____ **DATE:** __/__/20__

BUCKET LIST:

TARGET DATE: __/__/20__ **DONE** ✓ ☐

DATE COMPLETED: __/__/20__

WHERE:

HOW:

EXPERIENCE:

COMMENTS AND NOTES:

CATEGORY: _____ **DATE:** __/__/20__

BUCKET LIST:

TARGET DATE: __/__/20__   **DONE** ✓ ☐

DATE COMPLETED: __/__/20__

WHERE:

HOW:

EXPERIENCE:

COMMENTS AND NOTES:

CATEGORY:_____   **DATE:**__/__/20__

BUCKET LIST:

TARGET DATE: __/__/20__   **DONE** ✓ ☐

DATE COMPLETED: __/__/20__

WHERE:

HOW:

EXPERIENCE:

COMMENTS AND NOTES:

CATEGORY: _____ **DATE:** __/__/20__

BUCKET LIST:

TARGET DATE: __/__/20__   **DONE** ✓ [ ]

DATE COMPLETED: __/__/20__

WHERE:

HOW:

EXPERIENCE:

COMMENTS AND NOTES:

CATEGORY: _____ **DATE:** __/__/20__

BUCKET LIST:

TARGET DATE: __/__/20__   **DONE** ✓ [ ]

DATE COMPLETED: __/__/20__

WHERE:

HOW:

EXPERIENCE:

COMMENTS AND NOTES:

CATEGORY: _____ **DATE:** __/__/20__

BUCKET LIST:

TARGET DATE: __/__/20__   **DONE** ✓ [ ]

DATE COMPLETED: __/__/20__

WHERE:

HOW:

EXPERIENCE:

COMMENTS AND NOTES:

CATEGORY: _____ DATE:__/__/20__

BUCKET LIST:

TARGET DATE: __/__/20__   **DONE** ✓ ☐

DATE COMPLETED: __/__/20__

WHERE:

HOW:

EXPERIENCE:

COMMENTS AND NOTES:

CATEGORY:_____ **DATE:**__/__/20__

BUCKET LIST:

TARGET DATE: __/__/20__   **DONE** ✓ ☐

DATE COMPLETED: __/__/20__

WHERE:

HOW:

EXPERIENCE:

COMMENTS AND NOTES:

CATEGORY: _____ **DATE:** __/__/20__

BUCKET LIST:

TARGET DATE: __/__/20__   **DONE** ✓ ☐

DATE COMPLETED: __/__/20__

WHERE:

HOW:

EXPERIENCE:

COMMENTS AND NOTES:

CATEGORY:_____ **DATE:**__/__/20__

BUCKET LIST:

TARGET DATE: __/__/20__ **DONE** ✓ ☐

DATE COMPLETED: __/__/20__

WHERE:

HOW:

EXPERIENCE:

COMMENTS AND NOTES:

CATEGORY: _____ **DATE:** __/__/20__

BUCKET LIST:

TARGET DATE: __/__/20__   **DONE** ✓ [ ]

DATE COMPLETED: __/__/20__

WHERE:

HOW:

EXPERIENCE:

COMMENTS AND NOTES:

CATEGORY: _____ **DATE:** __/__/20__

BUCKET LIST:

TARGET DATE: __/__/20__   **DONE** ✓ [ ]

DATE COMPLETED: __/__/20__

WHERE:

HOW:

EXPERIENCE:

COMMENTS AND NOTES:

CATEGORY:_____ DATE:__/__/20__

BUCKET LIST:

TARGET DATE: __/__/20__   **DONE** ✓ [ ]

DATE COMPLETED: __/__/20__

WHERE:

HOW:

EXPERIENCE:

COMMENTS AND NOTES:

CATEGORY: _____ **DATE:** __/__/20__

BUCKET LIST:

TARGET DATE: __/__/20__ **DONE** ✓ [ ]

DATE COMPLETED: __/__/20__

WHERE:

HOW:

EXPERIENCE:

COMMENTS AND NOTES:

CATEGORY: _____ **DATE:** __/__/20__

BUCKET LIST:

TARGET DATE: __/__/20__   **DONE** ✓ ☐

DATE COMPLETED: __/__/20__

WHERE:

HOW:

EXPERIENCE:

COMMENTS AND NOTES:

CATEGORY:_____ **DATE:**__/__/20__

BUCKET LIST:

TARGET DATE: __/__/20__   **DONE** ✓ ☐

DATE COMPLETED: __/__/20__

WHERE:

HOW:

EXPERIENCE:

COMMENTS AND NOTES:

CATEGORY: _____ **DATE:** __/__/20__

BUCKET LIST:

TARGET DATE: __/__/20__   **DONE** ✓ [ ]

DATE COMPLETED: __/__/20__

WHERE:

HOW:

EXPERIENCE:

COMMENTS AND NOTES:

CATEGORY:_____ **DATE:**__/__/20__

BUCKET LIST:

TARGET DATE: __/__/20__   **DONE** ✓ ☐

DATE COMPLETED: __/__/20__

WHERE:

HOW:

EXPERIENCE:

COMMENTS AND NOTES:

CATEGORY: _____   **DATE:** __/__/20__

BUCKET LIST:

TARGET DATE: __/__/20__   **DONE** ✓ ☐

DATE COMPLETED: __/__/20__

WHERE:

HOW:

EXPERIENCE:

COMMENTS AND NOTES:

CATEGORY:_____ **DATE:**__/__/20__

BUCKET LIST:

TARGET DATE: __/__/20__ **DONE** ✓ ☐

DATE COMPLETED: __/__/20__

WHERE:

HOW:

EXPERIENCE:

COMMENTS AND NOTES:

CATEGORY: _____ **DATE:**__/__/20__

BUCKET LIST:

TARGET DATE: __/__/20__ **DONE** ✓ ☐

DATE COMPLETED: __/__/20__

WHERE:

HOW:

EXPERIENCE:

COMMENTS AND NOTES:

CATEGORY: _____ **DATE:** __/__/20__

BUCKET LIST:

TARGET DATE: __/__/20__   **DONE** ✓ [ ]

DATE COMPLETED: __/__/20__

WHERE:

HOW:

EXPERIENCE:

COMMENTS AND NOTES:

CATEGORY:_____ DATE:__/__/20__

BUCKET LIST:

TARGET DATE: __/__/20__   **DONE** ✓ [ ]

DATE COMPLETED: __/__/20__

WHERE:

HOW:

EXPERIENCE:

COMMENTS AND NOTES:

CATEGORY:_____ **DATE:**__/__/20__

BUCKET LIST:

TARGET DATE: __/__/20__   **DONE** ✓ ☐

DATE COMPLETED: __/__/20__

WHERE:

HOW:

EXPERIENCE:

COMMENTS AND NOTES:

CATEGORY: _____ **DATE:** __/__/20__

BUCKET LIST:

TARGET DATE: __/__/20__   **DONE** ✓ [ ]

DATE COMPLETED: __/__/20__

WHERE:

HOW:

EXPERIENCE:

COMMENTS AND NOTES:

CATEGORY: _____ **DATE:** __/__/20__

BUCKET LIST:

TARGET DATE: __/__/20__   **DONE** ✓ ☐

DATE COMPLETED: __/__/20__

WHERE:

HOW:

EXPERIENCE:

COMMENTS AND NOTES:

CATEGORY: _____ **DATE:__/__/20__**

BUCKET LIST:

TARGET DATE: __/__/20__   **DONE** ✓ ☐

DATE COMPLETED: __/__/20__

WHERE:

HOW:

EXPERIENCE:

COMMENTS AND NOTES:

CATEGORY:_____ **DATE:**__/__/20__

BUCKET LIST:

TARGET DATE: __/__/20__   **DONE** ✓ ☐

DATE COMPLETED: __/__/20__

WHERE:

HOW:

EXPERIENCE:

COMMENTS AND NOTES:

CATEGORY:_____ DATE:__/__/20__

BUCKET LIST:

TARGET DATE: __/__/20__   **DONE** ✓ [ ]

DATE COMPLETED: __/__/20__

WHERE:

HOW:

EXPERIENCE:

COMMENTS AND NOTES:

CATEGORY: _____ **DATE:** __/__/20__

BUCKET LIST:

TARGET DATE: __/__/20__   **DONE** ✓ [ ]

DATE COMPLETED: __/__/20__

WHERE:

HOW:

EXPERIENCE:

COMMENTS AND NOTES:

CATEGORY: _____ DATE:__/__/20__

BUCKET LIST:

TARGET DATE: __/__/20__   **DONE** ✓ ☐

DATE COMPLETED: __/__/20__

WHERE:

HOW:

EXPERIENCE:

COMMENTS AND NOTES:

CATEGORY:_____ **DATE:**__/__/20__

BUCKET LIST:

TARGET DATE: __/__/20__   **DONE** ✓ [ ]

DATE COMPLETED: __/__/20__

WHERE:

HOW:

EXPERIENCE:

COMMENTS AND NOTES:

CATEGORY:_____ **DATE:**__/__/20__

BUCKET LIST:

TARGET DATE: __/__/20__   **DONE** ✓ [ ]

DATE COMPLETED: __/__/20__

WHERE:

HOW:

EXPERIENCE:

COMMENTS AND NOTES:

CATEGORY:_____ **DATE:**__/__/20__

BUCKET LIST:

TARGET DATE: __/__/20__ **DONE** ✓ [ ]

DATE COMPLETED: __/__/20__

WHERE:

HOW:

EXPERIENCE:

COMMENTS AND NOTES:

CATEGORY: _____ **DATE:** __/__/20__

BUCKET LIST:

TARGET DATE: __/__/20__   **DONE** ✓ ☐

DATE COMPLETED: __/__/20__

WHERE:

HOW:

EXPERIENCE:

COMMENTS AND NOTES:

CATEGORY:_____ DATE:__/__/20__

BUCKET LIST:

TARGET DATE: __/__/20__   **DONE** ✓ [ ]

DATE COMPLETED: __/__/20__

WHERE:

HOW:

EXPERIENCE:

COMMENTS AND NOTES:

CATEGORY: _____ **DATE:**__/__/20__

BUCKET LIST:

TARGET DATE: __/__/20__ **DONE** ✓ [ ]

DATE COMPLETED: __/__/20__

WHERE:

HOW:

EXPERIENCE:

COMMENTS AND NOTES:

CATEGORY:_____ **DATE:**__/__/20__

BUCKET LIST:

TARGET DATE: __/__/20__   **DONE** ✓ [ ]

DATE COMPLETED: __/__/20__

WHERE:

HOW:

EXPERIENCE:

COMMENTS AND NOTES:

CATEGORY: _____ **DATE:** __/__/20__

BUCKET LIST:

TARGET DATE: __/__/20__   **DONE** ✓ ☐

DATE COMPLETED: __/__/20__

WHERE:

HOW:

EXPERIENCE:

COMMENTS AND NOTES:

CATEGORY:_____ DATE:__/__/20__

BUCKET LIST:

TARGET DATE: __/__/20__   **DONE** ✓ [ ]

DATE COMPLETED: __/__/20__

WHERE:

HOW:

EXPERIENCE:

COMMENTS AND NOTES:

CATEGORY:_____ **DATE:**__/__/20__

BUCKET LIST:

TARGET DATE: __/__/20__   **DONE** ✓ [ ]

DATE COMPLETED: __/__/20__

WHERE:

HOW:

EXPERIENCE:

COMMENTS AND NOTES:

CATEGORY:_____ DATE:__/__/20__

BUCKET LIST:

TARGET DATE: __/__/20__   **DONE** ✓ [ ]

DATE COMPLETED: __/__/20__

WHERE:

HOW:

EXPERIENCE:

COMMENTS AND NOTES:

CATEGORY: _____ **DATE:** __/__/20__

BUCKET LIST:

TARGET DATE: __/__/20__   **DONE** ✓ ☐

DATE COMPLETED: __/__/20__

WHERE:

HOW:

EXPERIENCE:

COMMENTS AND NOTES:

CATEGORY:_____ **DATE:**__/__/20__

BUCKET LIST:

TARGET DATE: __/__/20__   **DONE** ✓ ☐

DATE COMPLETED: __/__/20__

WHERE:

HOW:

EXPERIENCE:

COMMENTS AND NOTES:

CATEGORY: _____ **DATE:** __/__/20__

BUCKET LIST:

TARGET DATE: __/__/20__   **DONE** ✓ ☐

DATE COMPLETED: __/__/20__

WHERE:

HOW:

EXPERIENCE:

COMMENTS AND NOTES:

CATEGORY:_____   **DATE:**__/__/20__

BUCKET LIST:

TARGET DATE: __/__/20__   **DONE** ✓ ☐

DATE COMPLETED: __/__/20__

WHERE:

HOW:

EXPERIENCE:

COMMENTS AND NOTES:

CATEGORY: _____ **DATE:** __/__/20__

BUCKET LIST:

TARGET DATE: __/__/20__   **DONE** ✓ ☐

DATE COMPLETED: __/__/20__

WHERE:

HOW:

EXPERIENCE:

COMMENTS AND NOTES:

CATEGORY:_____ **DATE:**__/__/20__

BUCKET LIST:

TARGET DATE: __/__/20__   **DONE** ✓ ☐

DATE COMPLETED: __/__/20__

WHERE:

HOW:

EXPERIENCE:

COMMENTS AND NOTES:

CATEGORY:_____ **DATE:**__/__/20__

BUCKET LIST:

TARGET DATE: __/__/20__   **DONE** ✓ [ ]

DATE COMPLETED: __/__/20__

WHERE:

HOW:

EXPERIENCE:

COMMENTS AND NOTES:

CATEGORY:_____ **DATE:**__/__/20__

BUCKET LIST:

TARGET DATE: __/__/20__   **DONE** ✓ ☐

DATE COMPLETED: __/__/20__

WHERE:

HOW:

EXPERIENCE:

COMMENTS AND NOTES:

CATEGORY:_____ **DATE:**__/__/20__

BUCKET LIST:

TARGET DATE: __/__/20__   **DONE** ✓ ☐

DATE COMPLETED: __/__/20__

WHERE:

HOW:

EXPERIENCE:

COMMENTS AND NOTES:

CATEGORY:_____ **DATE:**__/__/20__

BUCKET LIST:

TARGET DATE: __/__/20__   **DONE** ✓ ☐

DATE COMPLETED: __/__/20__

WHERE:

HOW:

EXPERIENCE:

COMMENTS AND NOTES:

CATEGORY: _____ **DATE:** __/__/20__

BUCKET LIST:

TARGET DATE: __/__/20__ **DONE** ✓ ☐

DATE COMPLETED: __/__/20__

WHERE:

HOW:

EXPERIENCE:

COMMENTS AND NOTES:

CATEGORY:_____ DATE:__/__/20__

BUCKET LIST:

TARGET DATE: __/__/20__   DONE ✓ ☐

DATE COMPLETED: __/__/20__

WHERE:

HOW:

EXPERIENCE:

COMMENTS AND NOTES:

CATEGORY: _____   **DATE:** __/__/20__

BUCKET LIST:

TARGET DATE: __/__/20__   **DONE** ✓ ☐

DATE COMPLETED: __/__/20__

WHERE:

HOW:

EXPERIENCE:

COMMENTS AND NOTES:

CATEGORY: _____ **DATE:** __/__/20__

BUCKET LIST:

TARGET DATE: __/__/20__   **DONE** ✓ ☐

DATE COMPLETED: __/__/20__

WHERE:

HOW:

EXPERIENCE:

COMMENTS AND NOTES:

CATEGORY: _____ **DATE:** __/__/20__

BUCKET LIST:

TARGET DATE: __/__/20__ **DONE** ✓ ☐

DATE COMPLETED: __/__/20__

WHERE:

HOW:

EXPERIENCE:

COMMENTS AND NOTES:

CATEGORY: _____ **DATE:** __/__/20__

BUCKET LIST:

TARGET DATE: __/__/20__   **DONE** ✓ ☐

DATE COMPLETED: __/__/20__

WHERE:

HOW:

EXPERIENCE:

COMMENTS AND NOTES:

CATEGORY:_____ DATE:__/__/20__

BUCKET LIST:

TARGET DATE: __/__/20__ **DONE** ✓ ☐

DATE COMPLETED: __/__/20__

WHERE:

HOW:

EXPERIENCE:

COMMENTS AND NOTES:

Made in the USA
Monee, IL
04 May 2021